Aggie Savvy
Practical Wisdom from Texas A&M

Glenn Dromgoole

Aggie Savvy
Practical Wisdom from Texas A&M

Glenn Dromgoole

State House
Press

(Distributed by Texas A&M University Press)

Library of Congress Cataloging-in-Publication Data

Dromgoole, Glenn.
  Aggie savvy : practical wisdom from Texas A&M / Glenn
  Dromgoole.—1st ed.
     p. cm.
  ISBN-13: 978-1-880510-99-5 (hardcover : alk. paper)
  ISBN-10: 1-880510-99-5 (hardcover : alk. paper)
  1. Texas A & M University. 2. Texas A & M University
Anecdotes. I. Title.

  LD5309.D76 2005
  378.764'242--dc22

                                                    2005016572

Distributed by:
Texas A&M University Press
(800) 826-8911 • www.tamu.edu/upress

Printed in Canada

ISBN 1-880510-99-5

Book Designed by Rosenbohm Graphic Design

Grants

C. Harwell Barber '47
Raymond McDaniel Jr. '55
Bob J. Surovik '58

Photographs

Cover photograph by Dave McDermand
Dave McDermand: 6, 9, 14, 22, 25, 28, 44, 46, 48, 52, 60, 64, 72,
    76, 88, 92, 94, 96, 106
Allan Pearson: 16, 18, 24, 54, 56, 58, 66, 70, 74, 82
Sharon Aeschbach: 80, 86, 104, 110
Glen Johnson: 20, 38, 62, 84
Butch Ireland: 36, 50
Adam Beaugh: 30, 98
Kati Barrett: 10
Jim Lyle: 12
Larry Wadsworth: 90
Glenn Dromgoole: 7, 8, 34, 42, 68, 100, 102
The Big Event: 32, 40
Texas A&M Archives: 78, 108

Acknowledgments

Ashlee Dietrich '05
Bryan-College Station Eagle
The Battalion, Texas A&M
University Relations, Texas A&M
Agricultural Communications, Texas A&M
Texas A&M University Press

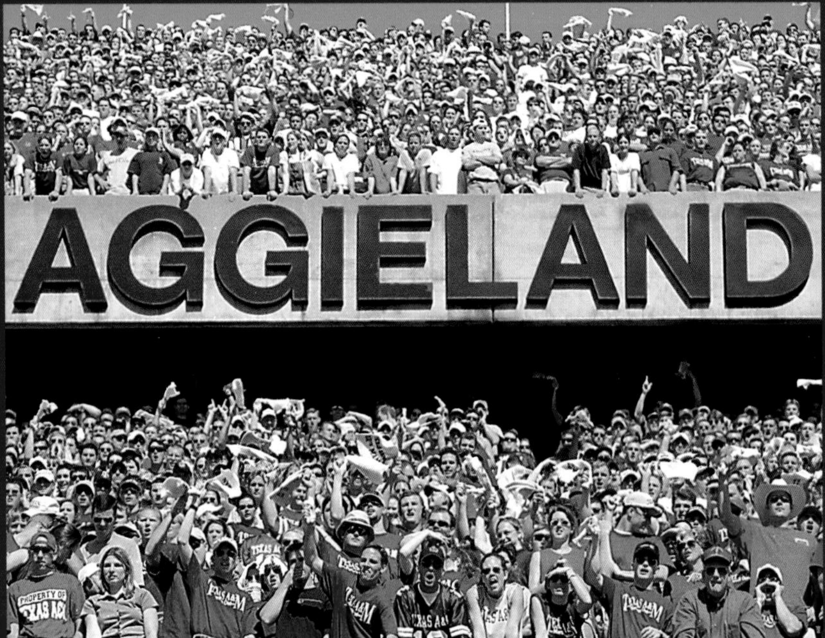
AGGIELAND

Introduction

Although Texas A&M has changed dramatically through the years as it evolved into a first-class university, it has managed to retain its distinctive cultural heritage and hold on to the Aggie Traditions which have defined and enriched the school and given it character and soul.

Aggies are unparalleled in their zeal to honor the past while embracing the future. Texas A&M is no longer the all-male, military, agricultural and engineering bastion that it started out to be, yet the Corps of Cadets remains a significant influence in student life and Aggies still yell "Farmers Fight" and sing the "Aggie War Hymn" at ball games. The Fighting Texas Aggie Band continues to stir passions with its precision marching to military compositions.

Traditions such as Aggie Muster, Yell Practice and Silver Taps are as important to today's Aggies as they

were to yesterday's. At the same time, new "traditions" such as the Big Event are gradually blended with the old to accommodate changing times and emerging sentiments.

When Aggies talk about the "Spirit of Aggieland," it is more than a school song. It is a sense of pride and purpose in what makes the school unique, an enduring experience, an abiding impression. Aggies are known for their fierce loyalty and devotion to A&M and to each other. Graduates do not become ex-Aggies after they leave Aggieland but rather "former students." They are expected to be Aggies the rest of their lives.

In words and pictures, *Aggie Savvy* celebrates that spirit and that uniqueness by focusing on the practical wisdom and life lessons—profound and trivial, philosophical and whimsical—that can be gleaned from the culture, the environment and the lore at Texas A&M.

Glenn Dromgoole '66

The world would
be a friendlier
place if everyone
said howdy.

Invest in a
good education.

Sing with gusto.

Respect the flag.

Make some noise.

Do your job and don't worry about who gets the glory.

Take time to
show respect
for those
who have
passed away.

Pass along
important
traditions.

Get plenty of exercise.

It's better to cram before an exam than after one.

Hope for a little good luck
and grace along the way.

Give something back to
your community.

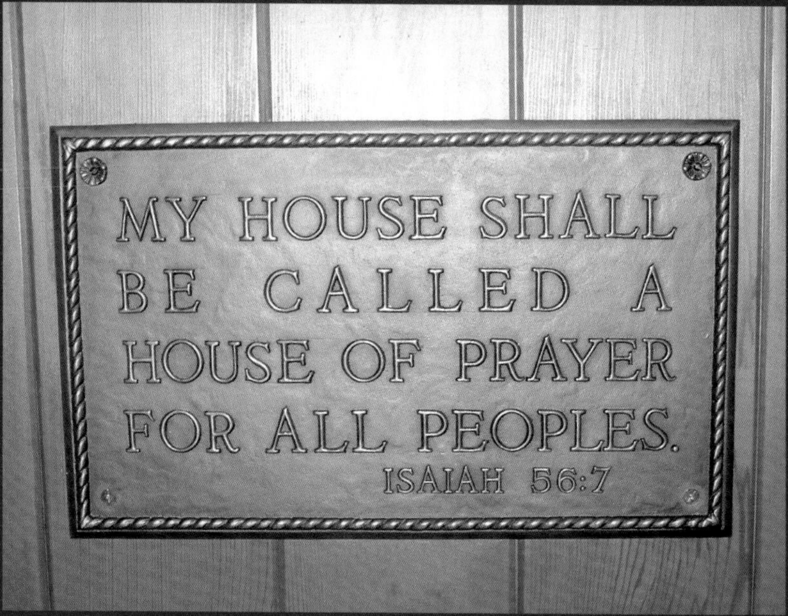
MY HOUSE SHALL
BE CALLED A
HOUSE OF PRAYER
FOR ALL PEOPLES.
ISAIAH 56:7

Nourish your faith and respect others' beliefs.

Yell for your team.

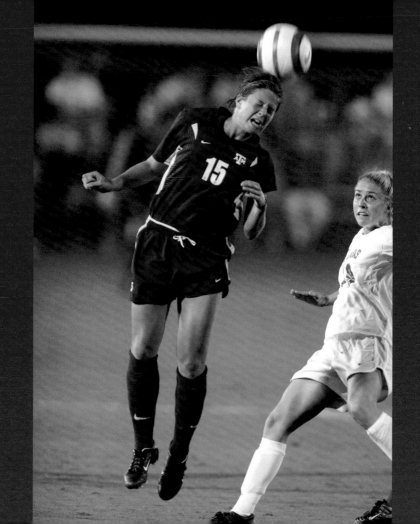

When in doubt, remember
to use your head.

Working together on a project is a good way to make lasting friendships.

A real leader has to make
tough decisions.

Honor those who gave their lives for their country.

Don't be afraid to get
your feet wet...

...or your hands dirty.

Stand up for
America!

Lead the way.

Be sure to
ask the right
question.

Learn from the masters.

A ring ought to stand
for something.

March to the right drummer.

Stay focused on the task
at hand.

Don't pass up the opportunity
to get a quick nap.

Treat animals with the respect they deserve.

Remember where you parked.

Whoop it up.

Give it all you've got.

Read more.

Wherever you are, find ways to build bridges.

WE'VE
BEEN

INSPIRED BY THE FIGHTING S

with RICHARD QUINE   ANN

NOAH BEERY, JR.   MARTHA O

HARRY DAVENPORT   WILLIAM F

EDGAR BARRIER   BOB MI

and BILL STERN

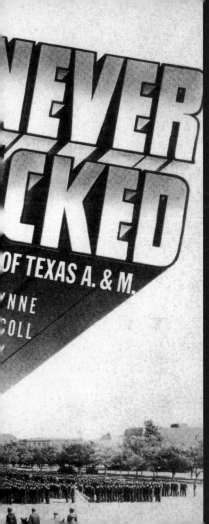

Never
give up.

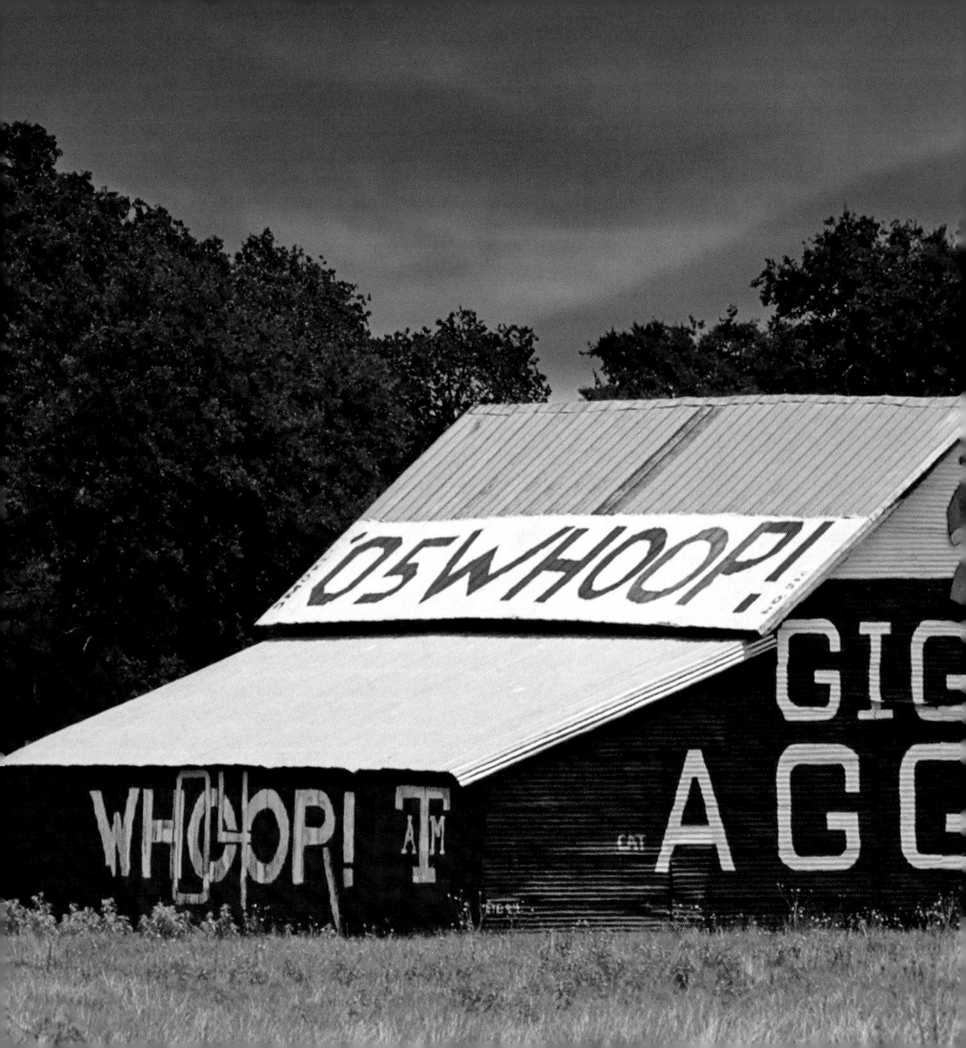

'05 WHOOP!
WHOOP!
GIG
AGG

Make a bold
statement.

Always strive
for excellence.

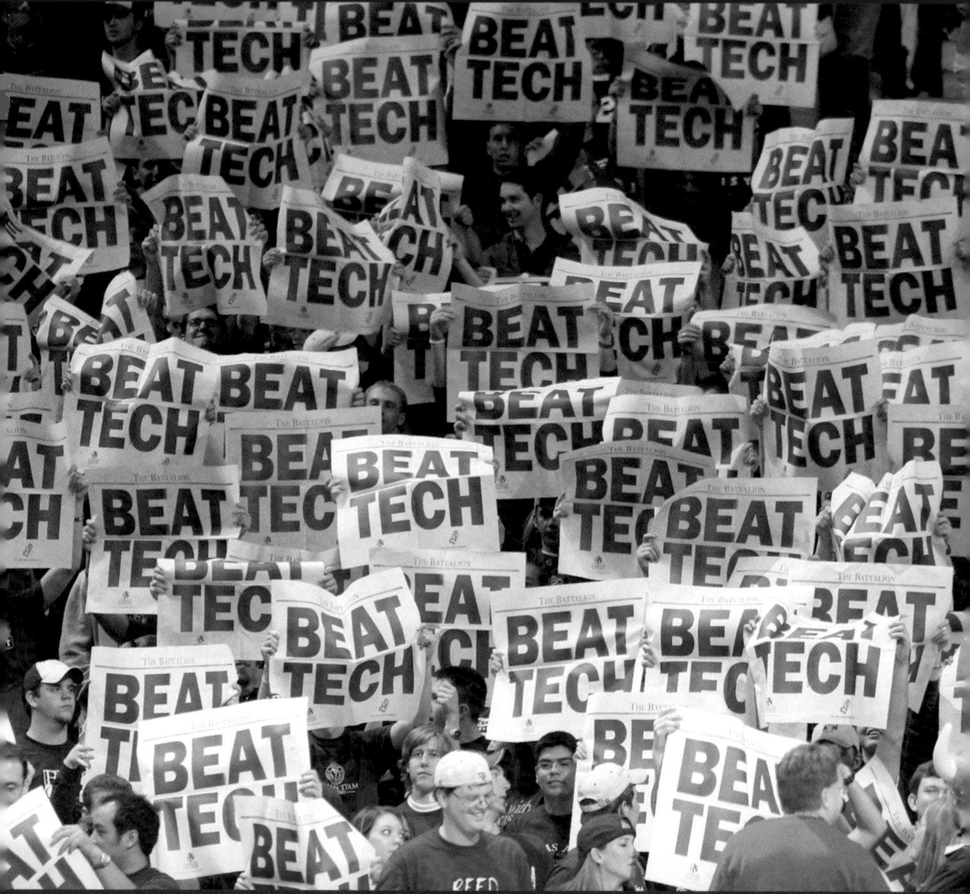
THE BATTALION
BEAT
TECH

Make your point clearly
and concisely.

Know when to
toot your own
horn...

...and when not to.

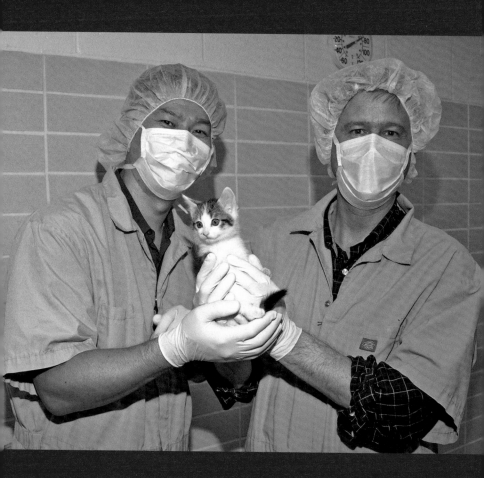

If you don't have a cat,
clone one.

Plan for the future.

Cast your own shadow.

Climb mountains,
even man-made ones.

Light up your corner
of the world.

Wear good boots.

To get where you're going,
it's important that you catch
the right bus.

No task is too
large if you get
enough people
to pitch in.

Get 'em while
they're young...

... and keep them
all their lives.

There's a spirit
can ne'er be told.

Notes

Page 8: Statue outside Kyle Field recognizes the spirit of the 12th Man.

Page 22: Aggie Muster on the Texas A&M campus.

Page 30: Students place pennies, even notes, on the statue of Lawrence Sullivan Ross in hope of a little extra luck on exams.

Page 32: The Big Event involves thousands of Aggies doing community service projects on one day.

Page 34: A plaque in All Faiths Chapel.

Page 42: Earl Rudder, '32, a World War II hero, led A&M through major changes during his tenure as president, 1959-70.

Page 46: Elephant Walk, a Texas A&M tradition since 1922.

Page 48: The Corps of Cadets March to the Brazos raises money for the March of Dimes.

Page 50: On Sept. 22, 2001, fans decked Kyle Field in red, white and blue while "Standing for America."

Page 54: The Century Oak on campus is a popular place for proposals.

Page 56: Former President George Bush often visits the A&M campus, which houses his Presidential library.

Page 66: Reveille VII is the First Lady of Texas A&M.

Page 78: The World War II propaganda movie "We've Never Been Licked" featured Texas A&M campus scenes and traditions.

Page 90: The first successful cloning of a cat was performed by College of Veterinary Medicine researchers in 2001.

Page 108: P.L. "Pinkie" Downs, Class of 1906, is credited with popularizing the thumbs-up "Gig'em Aggies" symbol.

Page 110: The Bonfire Memorial pays tribute to the Aggies killed and injured in 1999 while working on Bonfire and reflects the teamwork, belonging, tradition and dedication that are part of the Aggie Spirit that "can ne'er be told."